CAREERS IN

GRAPHIC ART AND DESIGN

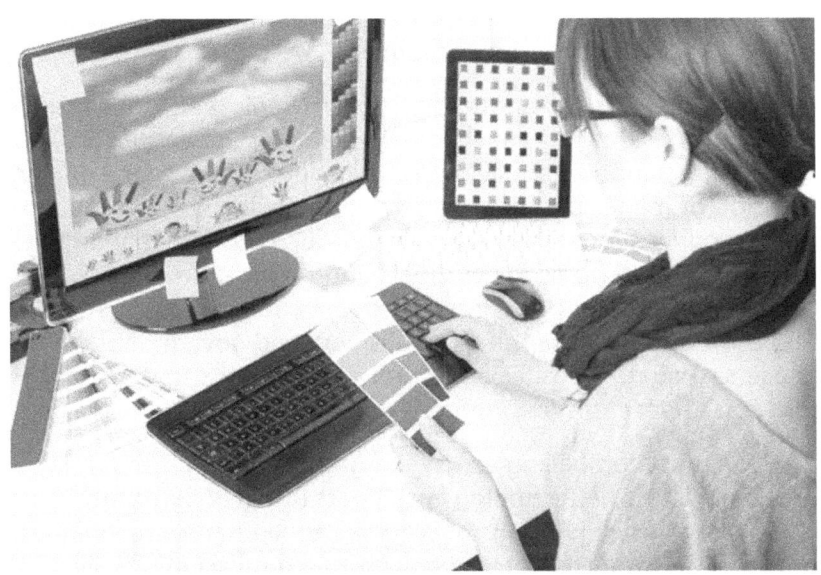

GRAPHIC DESIGN IS ONE OF THE MOST flexible careers imaginable. From the types of places where you can work to the different jobs that you can do, the combinations are nearly infinite. You can join the ranks of established Fortune 500 companies, or march to your own tune as a self-employed freelancer. You can work from your home office in your pajamas, or put on a suit and tie and direct an advertising agency. You can even make movies for Disney!

Graphic designers are the renaissance artists of the 21st century. The graphic designer is a true artist, drawing inspiration from everywhere – television shows, food, clothing styles, faraway places, nature, and interesting people. Unlike starving artists of days gone by, however, these highly skilled individuals are well paid to create art in the Digital Age. They influence every area of our culture, and continually have more and more input into every area of society. These artists are responsible for creating clothes, furniture, signs, websites, books, magazines, commercials, home appliances, cars, traffic signals, product packaging, the layout of city parks and tourist attractions, and even driverless cars. They deliver messages through visual concepts, designed to communicate ideas that inspire, inform, and captivate consumers.

Graphic designers use a variety of print, electronic, and video media to create the designs that meet commercial needs of employers and clients. Using computer applications, they develop the overall layout and design of magazines, newspapers, journals, corporate reports, and other publications. They also may produce promotional displays and marketing brochures for products and services, develop distinctive company brands, and create signs and signage systems (called environmental graphics) for business and government. They help users navigate websites and produce the credits that appear before and after television programs and movies.

One of the most compelling aspects of graphic design is that it is always changing. The technology used gets updated constantly. There are always new versions of software to learn, new techniques to apply, new strategies to try out. Getting a design job usually requires a four-year college or art school degree, but graduation is not the end of a designer's education. Lifelong learning is needed to succeed in this field.

The specialties of web design, animation, video entertainment, and user experience, are currently seeing the most job growth, but the whole industry is seeing an uptick. There is the potential to make nearly six figures in this career if you are highly skilled and choose a hot specialty. Most designers will not obtain that level of success, but every designer can build a rewarding and satisfying career. That could mean climbing the corporate ladder, working solo, or creating an independent agency or design studio.

If you are creative, love to learn, speak Adobe, and are handy with a keyboard and mouse, graphic design could be a good fit for your career.

WHAT YOU CAN DO NOW

YOU CAN START PREPARING FOR A career in graphic art while still in high school. You will naturally want to take as many art classes as possible, including sculpture, drawing, and painting. While it is true that classes that focus on hand-created art instead of computer-generated design do not directly teach you the skills you will need to master the graphic arts in the digital world. They will inspire and inform your creative process when you begin to work on the computer later. At the same time, they will also teach you essential basics, such as color theory, shape, perspective, and shadows. You will learn how to look at objects in a different way so that you understand how to recreate and manipulate them on a computer.

Most graphic art work today is done on computers, so any computer classes would be helpful. Become familiar with a range of computer graphics and design applications. The most widely used are the components of the Adobe Creative Suite, including Photoshop, Illustrator, InDesign, Premiere Pro, and Dreamweaver. If your school does not offer instruction in these programs, you will find classes somewhere in your community. Explore Adobe applications on their website at www.adobe.com/CreativeSuite. They offer special discounts for students.

Outside of the classroom, take a look at the extracurricular activities that your school offers and notice any that can boost your design skills. Join the yearbook, school newspaper, or school magazine. If your school has a website, volunteer to work on that. If not, offer to create one. Each of these activities will help you gain valuable experience creating layouts and using different digital software. Start gathering samples of your work. It is never too soon to start building a portfolio of your designs. You will need it for the college or art school admissions process, as well as job seeking later on.

Join professional associations as a student member to gain knowledge about the profession.

HISTORY OF THE CAREER

PEOPLE HAVE BEEN COMMUNICATING through pictures since civilization began. It may have started with animal drawings on cave walls in France, expanded to pictures on pottery, and accompanied works of literature as illustrations. You can find evidence of art dating back to 30,000 BC.

It seems as long as people have been writing, they have been pairing words with pictures. The two forms of communications are almost inextricably linked together, two sides of the same coin, two complementary ways to spread your message. In 2500 BC, the Egyptians used symbols called hieroglyphics to get their point across. Medieval manuscripts have been found with spaces left free so artists could fill them in with illustrations. Words and pictures just seem to go together. They did back then, and they do now, in a world of trademarks and logos and type fonts and other forms of graphic art.

Posters and signs have been around since ancient times too, serving then as advertisements in Roman markets and announcements of Greek athletes in the city's central meeting places.

When Johann Gutenberg developed his printing press in 1450, graphic design took a new turn into the world of print. Suddenly mass production was possible, and everything changed. Typography was born, and soon specialized artists were designing distinctive typefaces. People began to pay attention more closely to font size and differences in readability. Books, newspapers, and other printed announcements became more common, were produced more quickly, and were distributed to more people than ever. During the Industrial Revolution, type took center stage again, as mass-produced posters were used as advertising media.

The 19th century saw the birth of another integral part of the graphic arts – moving pictures. They can be seen as far back as

Eadweard Muybridge's galloping horse in 1887. Around the turn of the 20th century, films were less than a minute long, with one stationary camera recording the actors in a single take. In the early 1900s, more advanced camera work was introduced, with camera movement, and techniques like stop motion editing. G. A. Smith created the special effect reverse motion, and things in the film industry were turned on their heads. Animation took off too, with the help of Arthur Melbourne-Cooper and Edwin Stanton Porter. Film special effects and animations have come a significant way since then, as anyone who has ever seen a Pixar film or Matrix movie can tell you. It has spilled over into the world of computer technology, with much of the film creation now being done on the computer by talented graphic artists.

Some consider William Morris to be the father of modern graphics. Together with Dante Gabriel Rossetti and Burne-Jones, these three men started the group known as the Pre-Raphaelites, in the mid-19th century, establishing the principles behind modern graphic design.

Among the most famous of the graphic artists, were two men from the glamorous age of advertising in the 1930s – Raymond Leowy and William Golden. Leowy was the genius behind the logos of Shell, Greyhound bus, and Lucky Strike, while Golden is best known for the CBS logo.

Another turning point in the graphic arts was, of course, the introduction of the computer. It changed the way artists created things much like the printing press did. Now by using digital software, designers are able to incorporate different effects, which were for the first time easily changeable. If they did not like their design, they could simply start over without having spent anything but their time on the project. There would be no paper to throw away, no expensive supplies used in the making of their mock-ups. If money was spent in the process, it was spent on the technology itself or the invoice the designer gave to a client.

Programs like Photoshop and Illustrator were introduced, allowing anyone with access to them to create their own designs. People could change colors, add filters, adjust the size and shape, and rearrange elements of a design with the click of the mouse or a few keyboard shortcuts. The graphic arts became more accessible than ever – and easily mastered by anyone with a bit of patience or the money to spend on the software.

One of the biggest changes to the graphic arts that came about with the introduction of the computer, was the decline of print media and the increase in digital forms of advertising. Now every business has a website, and every website has someone who designed it. Logos are more important than ever, too, distinguishing professionals from amateurs. Interestingly enough, there are both professionals and amateurs when it comes to logo design. You can buy a simple logo for $5 now, or you can hire a highly trained and reputable graphic artist to create one for you for thousands of dollars. The difference is clearly evident – you get what you pay for!

WHERE YOU WILL WORK

GRAPHIC DESIGNERS GENERALLY WORK in studios where they have access to drafting tables, computers, and the software necessary to create their designs. Although many graphic designers work independently, those who work for specialized graphic design firms often work as part of a design team. Some designers telecommute, collaborating on projects or working with clients located around the world.

Almost a third of graphic designers are self-employed. These freelancers typically work from home. They may travel to meet with clients when necessary, though it is often possible to meet online using Skype or Google Hangouts. Regardless, the work itself is produced in a home-based workspace that consists of a desk or table, chair, computer, and a large monitor.

Many graphic designers work for creative agencies. The workspace at an agency is not much different from that in a home office, however, creative agencies are known for having immense personalities. There is often a party-like atmosphere designed to help overcome the drudgery and stress of deadlines while freeing the creative juices. There are often indoor game rooms, couches or nap rooms, and outdoor "play" areas. Dogs are welcome and sometimes kids are, too. Most have kitchens stocked with goodies and some even cater meals on a daily basis. The décor is likely fun and funkier than in other office environments, and the staff (almost all "creative types") will have their own eclectic accouterments to adorn their workspaces. Getting to work is also made less stressful, with many agencies providing a van for employees, outfitted with power outlets and Wi-Fi.

Many graphic designers work for just one employer, which typically means a corporation's marketing department. For these in-house designers, the corporation environment is quite different than that of a creative agency. These are traditional office spaces with desks, cubicles, and fluorescent lights. Unless the company is located somewhere near the Silicon Valley (or similar tech center), it will be all work all the time – no extreme Frisbee or breaks for cookies and milk.

Advertising agencies and newspapers have traditionally been the biggest employers of graphic designers. They are still good places for designers to seek employment, but there are now many other options. These include large retailers, public relations firms, web development companies, book publishers, engineering firms, recording studios, event planners, and even some government agencies, to name a few.

A small percentage of graphic designers work in the movie and television industry. These designers sometimes work in production houses, adding in the special effects to a film during post-production or animating sequences for stories. A lucky few work on famed locations such as Lucas Ranch and Pixar, but most are situated in small firms that handle a variety of work from TV commercials to industrial videos.

THE WORK YOU WILL DO

GRAPHIC DESIGNERS ARE VISUAL COMMUNICATORS. Their job is to use text and images to convey a client's or employer's message to a targeted audience. To accomplish this, they select the typefaces, size, color, and line length of headlines, headings, and content. They choose stock images or create originals photographs and illustrations. Then they decide how text and images will go together. When using text in layouts, graphic designers collaborate closely with writers who choose the words and decide whether the words will be put into paragraphs, lists, or tables. With images, text, and color, graphic designers can transform statistical data into visual graphics and diagrams, which can make complex ideas more accessible.

Although projects vary greatly, each one follows the same process – a process that is often invisible to the final viewer. It starts with a "brief," which identifies the needs of the client. This brief states a problem to be solved or a specific outcome to be achieved. The designer then collects information and analyzes it to determine the most effective solution. A successful outcome is not measured by how pretty it looks, but by how well the message is expressed and received. The fun part is, graphic designers can use literally any visual medium to give form to these directed communications. They select shapes, colors, typefaces, and illustrations for print design, websites, products of all sorts, and digital media. They can use photography, sound, and animation. They can use billboards, walls, or the faces of buildings. They can even use nothing at all, called "white space." Any technique and medium that can be used to get the message across is fair game.

There is an infinite variety of graphic design projects and the most successful designers have a specialty that sets their work apart. Every graphic designer, however, does most of these basic functions:

Meet with clients or the art director to determine the scope of the project

Discuss strategies on how to best reach the targeted audience

Determine the message the design should convey

Create images that identify a product or deliver a message

Develop illustrations and acquire photos

Select colors, text style, and layout

Produce hand-drawn or electronic sketches of the layout, followed by a mockup presented for approval

Present the design to clients or the art director

Incorporate changes that are recommended into the final design

Review designs for errors before printing or publishing them

Through every step of the process, the designer must consider the target market or audience, taking social and cultural considerations into account.

How much of the actual design work is completed by any one designer will depend on the size and type of employer. For example, a small retail chain might expect the designer to handle all design duties. All direction would come directly from the employer, or client. The designer could create flyers, product catalogs, and advertisements. Creating a distinctive logo or developing a website would also fall to the graphic designer.

The situation would be different for a graphic designer working in-house for a large corporation. This designer normally would meet with an art director to receive directions for any assigned project. Duties are typically limited to specific tasks, not the entire project. The designer might be responsible for selecting and editing photos from a product shoot, creating an original typeface, or reorganizing a website's navigation. It would be very unlikely that the same designer would undertake all these tasks.

Agency Designers

Interns

Most graphic designers work for an agency at some point in their career. In an agency setting, all designers follow the same career ladder. On the bottom rung is the intern, sometimes unpaid, though treated like a regular employee. Interns start out doing very simple tasks while learning the ropes. They often are relegated to menial jobs like making copies, fixing red-eye in photos, and note taking. In fact, there may be little to no real design work done during an internship.

Assistant Designers – Juniors

The next rung on the ladder is the assistant role. Assistant designers are also known as "juniors." This is a crucial step in a graphic designer's career as there will now be hands-on training that will be preparation for becoming a senior designer. Assistant designers learn these skills from someone already in that position. The work done by assistants is only slightly more advanced than the work done by interns, at least in the beginning. It is likely to include some actual design tasks, such as setting up photography equipment or making basic graphics. The assistant may also begin to interact with the client in limited capacities. Assistant designers usually work in a team of juniors that reports to a senior. Within the team, each junior designer may be responsible for a specific contribution such as color or photography.

Senior Designers

The next level up is a full designer, commonly known as a "senior." Senior designers interface with clients and are capable of completing most of the design work. They may also have assistants and interns working under them, to train and delegate tasks to.

As for the design tasks themselves, that will be dependent on the client's needs. It could be anything from designing website pages to YouTube channel backgrounds to a Facebook page. Agencies are notorious for doing everything but fixing the kitchen sink for a client – especially small agencies. At this level, graphic designers are also likely to be responsible for a number of project management chores, such as setting up deadlines and keeping team members on track for deliverables.

Creative Directors – Art Directors

Above senior designers are the creative directors, sometimes known as art directors. These are managers that keep the design team together. Creative directors are the big picture visionaries behind each project. They may also be the people who brought the clients to the agency in the first place. They do little design work themselves, but they oversee and critique what the other levels do before the clients see the final product.

In-House Designers

In-house designers are employed by a single client or company. They usually work in the marketing department, where they create promotional materials of all kinds. This may include making tweaks to an existing website, designing signage to be used at exhibitions, creating the layout of a digital newsletter that goes out to customers, producing industrial videos, or making banners and images for the company's blog. The amount of control the designer has over the creative process will depend on the size of the company and its marketing team. While there is some flexibility in this role, for the most part there have already been brand standards enacted. That means all designs must utilize the typefaces and colors that match the company's existing materials. The only exception is the rare occasion when a company decides to reinvent its brand.

Freelancers

A freelance graphic designer is essentially self-employed, able to negotiate and accept contracts from any company, organization, individual that needs work done. Generally, freelancers are hired on a per project basis. When the project is complete, a freelance graphic designer moves on to the next project, either with the same company or with someone else.

The assignment might be to create anything that a company may need that is based in art or graphics. It may be as simple as laying out a webpage design in Dreamweaver, editing a picture for a banner in Photoshop, or making a promotional video in Flash. It could be as large as developing an entire branding concept with a color palette, logo, and distinct look and feel.

Freelance graphic designers may have to do every part of the project, or they may be handed a small piece and told to execute it. They are often working as part of a team, but instead of meeting onsite, the team members would probably meet online. Putting together a team of freelancers like this means the company can pick and choose the most talented specialists from anywhere in the country.

Freelancers have to be highly skilled in order to attract ongoing work. They are often capable of working in more than one specialty and are adept in numerous kinds of software.

STORIES OF GRAPHIC DESIGNERS

I Own a Graphic Design Studio

"After 15 years of working in-house for companies both large and small, I decided to strike out on my own. I chose to establish a boutique-style studio because my customers love the personal attention that I offer versus a large ad agency. My forte is illustration so I now provide digital illustration for everything from web or print ads, to posters and Facebook covers.

Having my own studio is more exciting than being employed in-house because I get to work with such a diverse clientele. Just last month I contracted with a Roman Catholic Diocese, a modeling school, and a real estate broker with 17 offices. The clients may require very different services, but I start the process with each one in the same way. I conduct what I call a creative brief with clients, which allows me to collect valuable information that will help me make the finished product uniquely theirs. It is very important to listen carefully during these meetings. A great designer is a good listener first, a good artist second.

The best part of this work is the flexibility. I have chosen to work from my home because I need a flexible schedule to accommodate family responsibilities. The technology today allows me to do that. I can provide design services to clients all over the world. I can also expand my ability to provide high quality services that go beyond my own skills set by hiring freelance partners, like copywriters, photographers, SEO (search engine optimization) experts, and translators. These partners can be located anywhere so I'm not limited to the pool of talent in my backyard.

My advice to designers who might be thinking of going solo is to consider their strengths. In this situation, it is not enough to be a good designer. You must be a people person. You're not creating art for your own pleasure. It is all about the client. You must be able to understand the needs of the client. I truly love interacting with people, but not everyone does. If you can interweave your client's personality into the final product, you will have no trouble attracting a steady flow of contracts."

I Am a Junior Designer

"I work for an ad agency that provides services such as interactive web design, commercials, video editing, and events. There is some print design work, but that is slowly phasing out.

I started out as an unpaid intern here and was fortunate to be hired after only three months. I am still working my way up to be a senior designer, but I'm getting close. In the meantime, I enjoy my work very much, and every day I learn something new. I began with simple tasks like photo touch-up and color correction. That might mean taking people out of pictures or changing the color of a shirt, or removing blemishes. Basically, my job was to make everything look aesthetically pleasing.

Now I work closely with the art director to create compelling designs for PowerPoint presentations and websites. All of my work is done on the computer with Adobe programs such as Photoshop, Illustrator, and InDesign. I get new assignments almost every day. Some projects will take all week, while other times I will have three or four to complete in a single day.

The biggest challenge of this job is the fast pace. The deadlines are always tight and when a client decides to make a change to the final product at the last minute, it can be stressful. It can also be disheartening when those changes ruin a nice design, but the client is always right, so you have to accept it. The best part of my job is being creative. Sometimes I can't believe I get paid to do this because it is so much fun.

My advice to new designers is to intern somewhere before you choose your specialty. If you're still not sure, intern in more than one place. It will save you a lot of time in the long run."

I Am a Senior Designer

"I work at a digital design agency, specializing in brand and visual identity. Our client companies are mostly in the creative sector so I get to work on a variety of cool projects with a diverse range of creative people.

The best thing about my job is that there is no such thing as a typical day. There's always something new coming, and I look forward each morning to find out what it will be. I particularly enjoy new briefs and brainstorming sessions with the rest of the design team. Sharing ideas is so stimulating. I thrive on that kind of creativity. The working environment of design studios fosters free thinking. It's great to be interacting with like-minded people. I also like projects that I can sink my teeth into. Those are the ones that I do from start to finish. Being able to complete a project by myself is a really rewarding feeling.

The hardest part for me as a new designer was learning to take advice. I've learned to accept it, but when I was getting started and was exposed to clients for the first time, it was a shock. It never occurred to me that my projects wouldn't be accepted and appreciated first time around. It's really hard when you've put your creative soul into a new design, and the client picks it apart, and you have to make changes you don't agree will make it better. Most creative people tend to be sensitive, so this is a hard lesson to learn. A designer must learn that criticism is simply constructive feedback. It's just part of the process like erasing and redrawing a misplaced line.

I would advise new designers to stay on top of what is going on in the industry. Network and meet other creative professionals – even those who are not designers. You never know what opportunities may come of it."

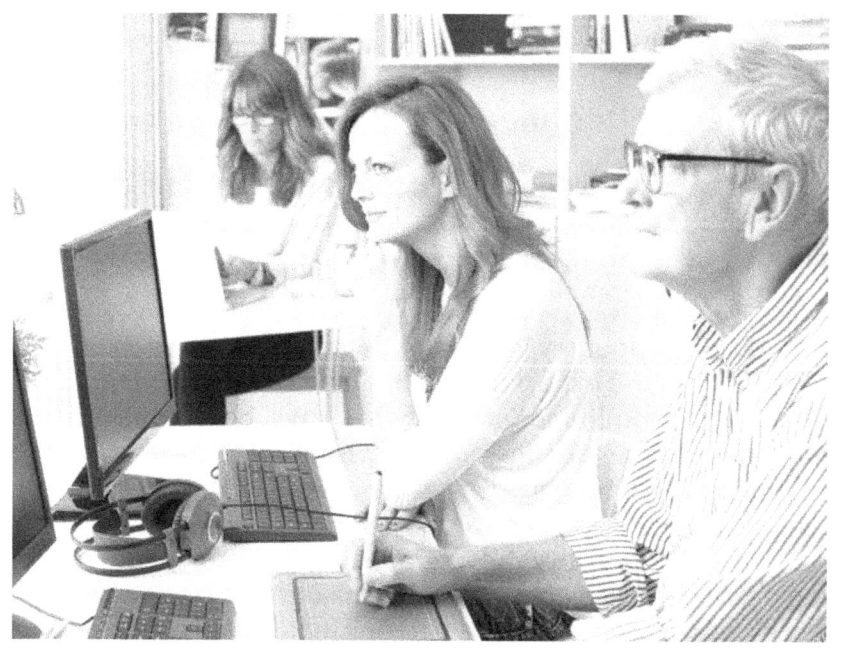

PERSONAL QUALITIES

BEING A SUCCESSFUL GRAPHIC designer requires a unique mix of creativity, skill, patience, excellent communications, and a touch of business savvy – all of which need constant nurturing for you to stay competitive in this profession.

Artistic ability is the most basic trait needed by all graphic artists and designers. Graphic artists have a natural talent for creating things and are inspired by the world around them. These professionals must be able to create designs that are artistically interesting and appealing to clients and consumers. This is not the same as creating art for art's sake. Graphic designers must be able to see their work from the consumer's point of view and ensure they are conveying the client's message in the most effective ways. Their creativity must go beyond choosing the attractive colors and shapes. Graphic designers must be able to think of new approaches to communicating ideas to consumers through unique designs that convey a memorable message on behalf of their clients.

People who work in the graphic arts can sketch, paint, and sculpt, but they are also very tech savvy. They know their way around a computer, its functions and programs. In general, they are quick to learn, and they adapt well to changes.

Communications skills are essential. Graphic designers must communicate with clients, customers, and other designers to ensure that their designs accurately reflect the desired message and effectively express information. Because of the client interaction involved in this profession, it is important that a graphic designer be good at face time with other people. This is particularly true for those who work as freelancers or in agencies. There will be client phone calls and meetings where you are expected to hear the feedback from the client and implement it. That feedback may seem harsh to the artistically sensitive, but it is essential to the process. For this reason, you must know how to take constructive criticism well. The most successful graphic designers are able to accept critiques, make the necessary changes, and deliver a final product that satisfies the clients.

Time management skills are important. Graphic designers often work on multiple projects at the same time, each with a different deadline. Those who excel in this career have developed a reputation for getting things out the door on time. If they don't, they run the risk of having trouble getting more work. Sticking to an agreed upon schedule is particularly important in an agency setting where the entire agency's reputation is on the line, and other members of the team need your piece of the puzzle to be completed before they can do theirs.

Multitasking is an essential skill. There are always either multiple clients or numerous projects from one client. It is necessary to be able to switch seamlessly between different projects, clients and tasks without skimping on quality or missing deadlines.

The ability to self-promote is vital to the success of freelancers. These self-employed professionals must be able to sell their products and services continuously. Without sales and new clients, there is no income.

ATTRACTIVE FEATURES

GRAPHIC DESIGN CAN BE A VERY rewarding career. This is one of the rare jobs where you actually have something to show people after you have completed the work. You get to point to it and say, "Look, I made this" as you build your portfolio.

Graphic designers have the chance to inspire people and change their minds by showing them different perspectives. Whether you create a well-designed website, a poster advocating social change, or an animated movie, your audience will see it and be forever changed. The change may be subtle or it may be profound. It may even be unnoticed by the viewer. As an artist, you are an "influencer," and you can take satisfaction in that.

The graphic arts provide the opportunity to be creative. It is a perfect outlet for experimenting, trying new things. It can be immensely satisfying, a canvas for ideas that need a place to sprout and live. They can live in a commercial, a mobile app, a clever T-shirt, an original auto design, or a digital comic book. The possibilities are endless, limited only by your imagination.

There is the chance for excellent earnings in graphic design. If you design your own art, you set your own prices and your business model. That means you can charge whatever you deem appropriate. If you freelance, you can set your own hourly or project-based rate, which is generally higher than the typical salary for the same work. If you are involved in the creation of something like a film, you may set up your contract to earn a percentage of the royalties. That means each time that film is shown or distributed, you could make additional money. Although most graphic designers earn less than $100,000 a year, those talented individuals who make it to the campuses of digital giants like Google, IDEO, Pixar, or Facebook, can earn several times that amount. Some get in on the ground floor of startups with compensation in the form of stock options that may be worthless or, after a successful public offering, worth enough for you to be set for life.

Graphic design offers almost unlimited potential for freedom and autonomy. You can choose to be a freelancer, start your own project and make your own art. You can also be your own boss and design your personal schedule based around how you like to work. It is also a career that can be location independent. This means you could choose to work from a beach in Thailand or a yacht in the Caribbean. Your workplace is your laptop and wherever there is Wi-Fi, you can send and receive work and payments.

If you decide you need the security and permanence of a regular job, there is employment with agencies or in-house with a single client. Then you would receive a weekly salary and benefits like paid vacations or healthcare.

Graphic designers get to work with very creative people of all types. Those who work in television or film also have the chance to be a part of an award-winning production and to collaborate with the other talent on board. For example, if you work at Disney or Pixar, you may be at the same wrap party when the project finishes as the lead star in the film.

UNATTRACTIVE FEATURES

THE CAREER OF GRAPHIC DESIGN PRESENTS some challenges. The first is being chained to a computer. While you may be inspired by the things you see around you in everyday life, eventually these will need to be translated into a digital format. That means spending many hours hunched over a keyboard. Eyestrain is common. Other possible side effects include carpel tunnel, fatigue, headaches, insomnia, and backaches.

The work is extremely detail oriented, a fact that can make it unsuitable for some artistic types. Choosing the right shade of blue for a pair of jeans in an ad on a website has the potential to take hours and hours. It is essential that the color on screen exactly match the real garment, or else customers will be disappointed. There are shadows and shading and overall composition to consider, which means a task that sounds simple is actually quite time-consuming and sometimes frustrating. There are a number of precision tools and techniques in every graphic arts program that require memorization and practice to learn how to use properly.

The field is constantly changing, mostly due to the development of new technologies and software. This means that what you know today could be outdated with the next version of Photoshop. Graduating from college with a design degree is not the end of your training, just the beginning. This is a profession that requires ongoing education to learn updates and advancements each time they are released, which can be several times a year.

Graphic designers have to be open to criticism. What seems beautiful to you may not look right to your client, who has a specific purpose in mind for the project. There is constant criticism in the art world – even more so in the field of graphic art. In the fine arts, artists have the last word on the pieces they create, even if no one else agrees with their vision. In graphic arts, however, the client is always right. That fact can be hard for some artists to swallow.

While it has the potential to be financially rewarding, those new to the field of graphic design often start out earning little more than minimum wages. Graphic designers may have to do a significant amount of work to build up a portfolio to get people to hire them in the first place, and much of that work will be unpaid. It is the age-old dilemma of beginners in any career: you have to demonstrate that you have done work for other clients before anyone will hire you, but how can you show what you are capable of if nobody will give you a chance? This can be very frustrating for people just starting out. It can only be overcome through determination and perseverance.

EDUCATION AND TRAINING

IN GENERAL, IT TAKES AT LEAST A bachelor's degree to land a professional job in graphic design. Graphic artists, whose work is truly fine art created in a graphic or digital medium, can get started with less formal training. Their creative education may vary from being self-taught, to obtaining a certificate from a technical college, to studying graphic arts in a two-year college program.

You could attend a liberal arts college or a conservatory of art and design. Four-year graphic design programs start with the basics and focus on traditional art forms. First year classes typically include drawing, studio art, sculpture, visual foundations, and art history.

Second year students take foundational graphic arts classes such as introduction to graphic design, introduction to typography, design principles, and basic 3-dimensional design. Classes in graphic design software are required at this point. By the end of the second year, students are expected to demonstrate proficiency in the most common computer programs: Photoshop, Illustrator, Dreamweaver, After Effects, Acrobat, Premiere, Quark, and InDesign.

Year three has students learning the more intricate ins and outs that will enhance their skill sets. Courses include multimedia design, print design, and graphic design for television and film. An increasing number of programs are also offering mobile and responsible design – this is what makes a website look great across multiple platforms such as laptops, tablets, and cell phones.

During the senior year, the training emphasizes actual job-related skills such as corporate identity design and branding, or advertising design. By now, most students have determined what type of graphic design work they want to specialize in, so they can pick and choose their own classes to match their interests. For example, someone looking to work in a production house on television or film would choose advanced courses in animation, 3D modeling, and special effects. Someone wanting to create websites for businesses would focus on web design, coding, and user experience. Those who have not settled on a particular career path can take this time to get a taste of illustration, photography, book design, computer animation, computer imaging, digital video, and screen printing.

Although not required for graduation, students should consider taking additional classes in writing, marketing, and business. These are obviously useful for those wanting to become self-employed or freelancers, but they can also help designers work effectively on project teams.

Throughout the four years of college, students are expected to build a professional portfolio of their designs. This means collecting examples of their best work from classroom projects, internships, and other experiences. Portfolios of seniors are expected to demonstrate that they have acquired adequate knowledge and skills during their four years in class. The same portfolio will be needed when applying for jobs and bidding on projects, although of course you will update it with professional samples as you finish them.

Graphic art and design programs are offered at colleges all over the country. The National Association of Schools of Art and Design accredits about 300 colleges. Most schools offer instruction in studio arts, computerized design, commercial graphics production, printing techniques, and website design.

The field of graphic design is always changing. Graphic designers must keep up with new and updated computer graphics and design software either through self-education or through formal software training programs. These programs are offered through professional associations such as the American Institute For Graphic Arts (AGA) and The Graphic Artists Guild.

EARNINGS

THE AMOUNT OF MONEY YOU CAN EARN as a graphic designer can vary greatly. A designer's total income will be based on many factors, including geographic location, the specialty field, the type of employer, and years of experience within the field.

Overall, the average annual earnings are about $45,000. The lowest paid earn less than $30,000, and the highest earners top out at about $80,000. Those who work in advertising agencies at the mid-level can make around $50,000 annually, while senior level executives make around $65,000 a year and directors around $90,000 in salary per year.

A typical starting salary for a new graphic designer is about $25,000 a year. This can be as an intern, as a freelance designer, or in a variety of entry-level positions. It is important for beginners to note that graphic design is one of those industries where experience – as demonstrated by your portfolio – is the most important factor in getting hired. Therefore, the best thing a low paid beginner can do is to start creating good work. Even if you are designing without pay (which you might be doing if your first job is an internship), the more good work you produce, the quicker you will advance.

For salaried designers, print design is by far the most common area of employment in the graphic design world. Print designers with a few years of experience earn about $40,000 a year on average. The next largest area of employment is in advertising and public relations. AD/PR designers earn between $35,000 and $50,000 a year. Graphic designers employed by software companies work on video games and design the user interface (UI) for computer programs. These designers enjoy average salaries of $50,000 to $65,000 a year.

The highest earnings are reserved for the top designers. These are people like senior designers working for companies like Apple, Coke, and Google. Their compensation easily exceeds six figures in salary alone, plus they often have additional sources of revenue such as shares of stock and personal freelance work.

Earnings are quite different for graphic designers who choose to freelance. The hourly fees for graphic designers vary wildly from as low as $5 per project on sites like Fiverr to $250 per hour for someone with a well-established reputation who consistently delivers incredible work. A mid-level freelancer typically earns around $50 an hour. Hourly earnings are based on time spent actually working on the project itself, and does not take into account any time spent obtaining contracts. This can be significant when a designer is just starting out. In fact, a beginner will likely spend 90 percent of the time trying to get work. That is time that will not be paid for. As the career progresses, the freelancer will gain more and more work from referrals and repeat clients, which greatly reduces the amount of unpaid time.

OPPORTUNITIES

THERE ARE AROUND 250,000 GRAPHIC designers in the US, working at least part time in the profession. This number is expected to grow at a rate of 10 percent in the United States, which is about average for all occupations. Competition is high if you do not specialize in one particular field. Most of the new available positions are in the web, animation, and video entertainment markets. Still, this industry is in need of fresh talent, and designers with unique and new ideas to offer are in demand.

Job opportunities for graphic designers used to be quite limited. There were advertising agencies and newspapers, and that was about it. It was generally considered a highly specialized niche career, one that was technical in nature, and not artistic at all. "Real" artists looked down on the profession, and unfairly judged those who entered the field for "selling out." Times have changed in a short time, and although ad agencies are still a good source of job opportunities, today there are many more avenues for graphic designers to pursue.

The biggest change in the graphic design job market is the trend towards hiring in-house designers, rather than using an outside ad agency. Retail stores and corporations have found it more cost effective to keep a staff of designers, however small, on the payroll. They have also found they get better results when projects do not have to be filtered through the layers of management that plague most agencies. Instead, in-house designers are focused solely on their one employer, the store or corporation. This concentration on the employer's brand promotes messages that are more on-point and highlights the particular company's culture seamlessly across all materials. It minimizes the ad agency's tendency to generalize and muddy the message. Ironically, the best way for graphic designers to compete for these in-house jobs is to have a portfolio that includes agency work.

One of the fastest growing areas for graphic designers is public relations. Similar to ad agencies, public relations firms are in the business of promotion. Instead of a product or service, though, they promote people. The two main types of clients here are celebrities (which include politicians) and events. In this increasingly celebrity crazed society, graphic designers are needed more than ever to produce promotional material for all media. These agencies look for designers with a wide range of skills – print, web presentations with Flash, video clips for the Internet and TV, CD covers, book covers, logos, trademarks, and everything else that can propel the subject into the limelight.

There are countless freelance and salaried print media designers. According to some estimates, there will be over 300,000 employed graphic designers within a decade. Print designers are needed to create everything from product packaging to business cards. The competition here is strong, however, it is easily counter balanced by the high level of demand. Due to this demand, print is where most graphic designers start their careers. Although it may seem as though print is disappearing, publications like magazines, books, and newspapers are alive and well – and always in need of graphic designers. Only the method of delivery has changed. Graphic designers who want to work for publishers need to know more than layout and typography. Their work will likely be concentrated in document production and website building.

The hottest area for graphic designers is known as "user experience," also called UI (user interface), UXD or UED (user experience design). User experience design revolves around the interaction between a customer (user) and a product. The goal of the UI designer is to enhance user satisfaction and loyalty by improving the usability or ease of use, and pleasure provided by the product. The result of the designer's work may not be clearly visible when it is done well, but when it is done poorly (or not at all), it is very obvious. For example, Apple products are known for being highly "user friendly." That is not by accident. In fact, constant work goes into making Apple products so easy to use that a manual would be superfluous. Conversely, it is easy to spot any website with bad UI. It probably has pages that take forever to load, colors that make the text hard to read, confusing navigation, and Flash overdose. User experience design is a highly multidisciplinary field, incorporating aspects of visual arts, anthropology, computer science, cognitive science, psychology, and of course, graphic design.

GETTING STARTED

BEFORE YOU CAN BEGIN YOUR JOB SEARCH, you need to determine what type of employer you want to work for. There is a wide variety of businesses that employ graphic designers. Each one will be looking for a specific type of design. Once you understand that, you can get ready to present yourself and your work in a portfolio. Your first portfolio should include only your very best work. Choose samples that clearly match the prospective employer's needs.

You will also need a résumé. This should not be the standard document used by every other job seeker. For the design applicant, a résumé provides a unique opportunity to make an individual design statement. The typographic design should reflect your skill and ability.

The next step is to figure out where you want to apply. Your school should have a placement office where you will find active job leads. This is where recruiters for large agencies and other organizations regularly turn to when seeking new talent for open design positions.

Visit your school library. There you will find design periodicals and annuals. These publications are great resources as they contain help wanted listings, usually nationwide. You can also get a list of your school's alumni. Contact those in the geographic area where you want to work. You will be surprised how willing alumni can be to help recent graduates get started.

Looking for a job is a serious networking activity. Start with your peers. Think of them as your supporters and collaborators, rather than the competition. The project that someone passes on due to a busy schedule or a short budget can be a project that is a good fit for you. Every project, no matter how small, adds another piece to your portfolio, which eventually can open doors to bigger and better opportunities.

Another way to build your network and add solid work to your portfolio is to sign up for volunteer projects. Offer your design skills to charities and other nonprofit organizations in your community. You will quickly have more work than you need. While there may be no pay, these projects could potentially lead to both fee-paying work and employment.

Internships also open doors. An internship with a good design studio or at an in-house department can offer valuable experience, as well as contacts. You will get to show off your skills and commitment, and possibly it will lead to a full-time paid position.

Create an online presence. These days prospective employers expect to see that you have your own website or active blog. At the very least, you can use an online portfolio service like Behance or Carbonmade. They are free and easy to use, so there is no excuse for not having an online presence.

You should already be a member of at least one good design organization. Now is the time to take advantage of the benefits these organizations offer, such as the chance to rub virtual (and real) shoulders with the who's who in the industry. The networking opportunities are invaluable. Soak up all the knowledge and advice you can, build your network, and you will soon have work lined up for the rest of your career.

ASSOCIATIONS

■ **American Institute of Graphic Arts**

http://www.aiga.org

■ **The Graphic Artists Guild**

www.graphicartistsguild.org

■ **The International Council of Graphic Design**

Associations (Icograda)

http://www.icograda.org

■ **Society for Experiential Graphic Design**

http://www.segd.org

■ **National Association of Schools of Art and Design**

http://nasad.arts-accredit.org

PERIODICALS

■ **Layers Magazine**

http://layersmagazine.com

■ **Print**

http://www.printmag.com

■ **I.D. Magazine**

www.id-mag.com/GeneralMenu/

■ **HOW Design**

http://www.howdesign.com

■ **Communication Arts Magazine**

http://www.commarts.com

WEBSITES

■ **Behance**

http://www.behance.net

■ **Carbonmade**

http://www.carbonmade.com

■ **Fiverr**

http://www.fiverr.com/categories/graphics-design

■ **RIT Design Archives**

http://library.rit.edu/gda

■ **Rhode Island School of Design (RSDI)**

http://www.risd.edu

■ **Typophile**

http://typophile.com/typeid

■ **Rochester Institute of Technology (RIT)**

http://rit.edu

■ **Kuler**

https://kuler.adobe.com/create/color-wheel

■ **Skillshare**

http://www.skillshare.com

www.ingramcontent.com/pod-product-compliance
Lightning Source LLC
Chambersburg PA
CBHW070755180526
45168CB00004B/1629